UNRAVELING THE SHINING

A Deep Dive into Kubrick's Masterpiece

Sharon B. Kaufmann

TABLE OF CONTENT

Chapter 1: The Shining: From Novel to Screen

Stephen King's terrifying story was given new life by Kubrick's imaginative direction. Stephen King's novel "The Shining" explored the terrifying and paranormal activities that surrounded the remote Overlook Hotel. When Stanley Kubrick took on the project to transform this literary work into a cinematic masterpiece, he brought his unique directorial vision to the forefront, diverging significantly from King's original storyline to create a narrative that delved into the psyche of its characters and the terror of isolation.

Kubrick's adaptation is noted for its departure from the novel's portrayal of Jack Torrance's character and its exploration of themes of madness and familial breakdown. Kubrick's choice to focus on psychological horror rather than supernatural elements allowed him to explore deeper themes of isolation and the disintegration of sanity, a decision that has been both celebrated and criticized by fans of King's original work.

One of the most debated aspects of Kubrick's adaptation is the portrayal of the Overlook Hotel itself. In the novel, the hotel serves as a malevolent entity that gradually corrupts its inhabitants, while in Kubrick's film, it becomes a vast, empty labyrinth that amplifies the characters' isolation and descent into madness. This shift in focus from supernatural horror to psychological terror created a chilling atmosphere that has resonated with audiences for decades.

Despite initial mixed reactions from both critics and fans of the novel, Kubrick's "The Shining" has since become a classic in the horror genre, praised for its innovative cinematography, haunting atmosphere, and iconic performances. The film's legacy continues to grow, with subsequent generations of filmmakers and horror enthusiasts citing it as a major influence on their work.

In this chapter, we will explore the evolution of "The Shining" from novel to screen, examining the creative decisions Kubrick made, the controversies surrounding the adaptation, and the film's impact on both popular culture and the horror genre. Join us as we delve into the labyrinthine depths of the Overlook Hotel and unravel the mysteries of Kubrick's cinematic vision.

Chapter 2: The Cinematic Techniques of Stanley Kubrick

Stanley Kubrick's directorial style in "The Shining" is renowned for its meticulous attention to detail and innovative use of cinematic techniques to create a deeply unsettling atmosphere. From the moment the camera begins to glide through the haunting corridors of the Overlook Hotel, Kubrick establishes a sense of unease that permeates the entire film.

Steadicam and Tracking Shots:
The steadicam, used by filmmaker/operator Garrett Brown in "The Shining," was one of the most innovative aspects of Kubrick's technique. With the use of this technology, characters could be tracked through the vast and intricate sets of the Overlook

Hotel in a fluid and seamless manner. The famous tracking shot of Danny Torrance riding his tricycle down the corridors not only serves to establish the vastness of the hotel but also creates a sense of inevitability and impending doom.

Symmetrical Framing and Composition:
Kubrick's compositions in "The Shining" are often characterized by their symmetry and meticulous framing. Symmetrical compositions, where elements of the frame are balanced on either side of the screen, create a sense of order and stability that is juxtaposed with the unsettling events unfolding within the narrative. This deliberate use of symmetry enhances the film's visual appeal while also contributing to its sense of unease and psychological tension.

Use of Color and Lighting:
Color plays a crucial role in establishing mood and atmosphere in "The Shining." Kubrick employed a distinct color palette throughout the film, with

vibrant shades of red, blue, and gold dominating different scenes. The use of color not only underscores the psychological states of the characters but also serves symbolic purposes, such as the use of red to signify danger or the supernatural presence within the hotel.

Sound Design and Music:

Sound design and music are integral components of Kubrick's cinematic technique in "The Shining." The eerie and dissonant score composed by Wendy Carlos and Rachel Elkind adds to the film's sense of unease and impending dread. Kubrick also used silence strategically, allowing moments of quiet to amplify tension and create a sense of isolation within the vast, empty spaces of the Overlook Hotel.

Visual Effects and Practical Effects:

While "The Shining" is primarily known for its psychological horror and atmosphere, Kubrick also incorporated subtle visual effects and practical effects to enhance the film's supernatural elements.

The use of practical effects, such as the elevator of blood or the ghostly apparitions that haunt the hotel, adds a visceral and tangible quality to the film's horror elements.

Chapter 3: Character Study:

Jack Torrances:

Jack Torrance, portrayed by Jack Nicholson, is at the heart of the psychological horror in Stanley Kubrick's "The Shining." A struggling writer and recovering alcoholic, Jack takes on the role of winter caretaker at the remote Overlook Hotel, hoping to find solitude and inspiration for his writing. But as the movie progresses, it becomes clearer how supernatural forces and his own inner demons are driving Jack's spiral into madness.

Initial Optimism and Fragile Stability:

At the beginning of the film, Jack appears optimistic about his new job and the opportunity to reconnect with his family. His interactions with his wife Wendy and son Danny initially suggest a desire to be a loving husband and father, despite his troubled past. Nicholson portrays Jack with a charismatic charm that quickly gives way to underlying tension and unease.

The Influence of the Overlook Hotel:

As Jack settles into his role as caretaker, the malevolent influence of the Overlook Hotel begins to take hold. Kubrick subtly layers the hotel's supernatural presence with Jack's psychological unraveling, blurring the lines between external forces and internal demons. The hotel's haunted history and the isolation of the winter setting exacerbate Jack's vulnerabilities, fueling his descent into madness.

Transformation into an Antagonist:

Jack's transformation from a struggling writer to a menacing antagonist is a testament to Nicholson's nuanced performance and Kubrick's direction. As the film progresses, Jack's behavior becomes increasingly erratic and violent, culminating in iconic scenes of terror and insanity. Jack, as portrayed by Nicholson, gradually loses control and devolves into a primitive state of madness, driven by the hotel's evil influence and his own unbridled ambition.

Complex Relationships:

Central to Jack's character study are his relationships with Wendy and Danny. His interactions with Wendy, portrayed by Shelley Duvall, oscillate between tenderness and explosive anger, reflecting the volatile nature of their fractured marriage. Jack's relationship with Danny, portrayed by Danny Lloyd, is fraught with tension and fear as Jack becomes increasingly obsessed with the hotel's dark secrets and Danny's psychic abilities.

Symbolism and Psychological Themes:

Jack Torrance serves as a symbolic representation of the film's exploration of isolation, madness, and the cyclical nature of violence. Kubrick's adaptation emphasizes Jack's internal struggle with identity and agency as he becomes a pawn in the hotel's malevolent machinations. The character's journey resonates with broader themes of familial trauma and the destructive power of unchecked ambition, making Jack Torrance a quintessential figure in the annals of horror cinema.

Chapter 4: The Overlook Hotel

A Character Itself:

In Stanley Kubrick's "The Shining," the Overlook Hotel transcends its role as a mere setting and becomes a character in its own right—a malevolent presence that looms over every frame of the film. From its grandiose architecture to its eerie emptiness, the hotel serves as a physical manifestation of the supernatural forces that haunt its corridors and the psychological unraveling of its inhabitants.

Labyrinthine Corridors and Design:

The Overlook Hotel is depicted as a vast and labyrinthine maze of corridors, rooms, and secret passages. Kubrick's use of expansive sets and intricate set design creates a sense of disorientation and foreboding, emphasizing the hotel's isolation and the characters' entrapment within its walls. The layout of the hotel, with its repeated motifs and mirrored symmetry, reflects the film's themes of repetition and cyclical patterns.

Symbolism and Haunted History:

Throughout the film, the Overlook Hotel is imbued with symbolism and a haunted history that mirrors the characters' psychological states. Rooms such as Room 237, where supernatural encounters occur, and the ballroom, where ghostly apparitions come to life, serve as focal points of the hotel's malevolent influence. The hotel's ominous presence is heightened by Kubrick's use of lighting, sound design, and visual effects to create an atmosphere of dread and uncertainty.

The Shifting Architecture:

One of the most unsettling aspects of the Overlook Hotel is its shifting architecture and the sense of spatial disorientation it evokes. Kubrick manipulates the layout of the hotel throughout the film, with rooms and hallways appearing and disappearing, adding to the characters' confusion and paranoia. This manipulation of space blurs the boundaries between reality and hallucination, reinforcing the film's exploration of madness and the supernatural.

Impact on Characters:

The Overlook Hotel exerts a profound influence on the characters of "The Shining," exacerbating their inner turmoil and driving them toward madness. For Jack Torrance, the hotel becomes a source of inspiration and obsession, fueling his descent into violence and insanity. Wendy and Danny Torrance, meanwhile, are isolated within the hotel's vast emptiness, vulnerable to its malevolent forces, and haunted by its dark secrets.

Cinematic Representation:

Kubrick's portrayal of the Overlook Hotel is a masterclass in atmospheric filmmaking, using visual and auditory cues to evoke a sense of dread and foreboding. The hotel's design, from its opulent interiors to its ominous exterior, reflects Kubrick's meticulous attention to detail and his ability to create an immersive cinematic experience. Each room and corridor of the hotel serve as a canvas for Kubrick's exploration of horror and psychological tension, leaving a lasting impression on audiences.

Chapter 5: Themes of Isolation and Madness

At the heart of Stanley Kubrick's "The Shining" lies a profound exploration of isolation and madness. themes that permeate the film's narrative and underscore its psychological horror.

Isolation in the Winter Setting:
The film is set in the isolated and snowbound Overlook Hotel during the winter months, a setting that exacerbates the characters' sense of isolation and confinement. Kubrick's use of the expansive hotel grounds, surrounded by snow-covered landscapes and desolate forests, underscores the characters' physical and psychological isolation. This isolation serves to heighten the film's atmosphere of dread and uncertainty, trapping the

characters within the confines of the hotel and cutting them off from the outside world.

Psychological Unraveling:

As the film progresses, the characters of "The Shining" experience a gradual unraveling of their sanity and sense of self. Jack Torrance, in particular, succumbs to the hotel's malevolent influence and his own inner demons, descending into a state of violent madness. Kubrick's portrayal of Jack's psychological deterioration is marked by moments of intense paranoia, hallucinations, and a loss of grip on reality, illustrating the destructive power of isolation and obsession.

Cabin fever and Claustrophobia:

The hotel's labyrinthine corridors and claustrophobic interiors contribute to a sense of cabin fever that pervades the film. Kubrick manipulates space and perspective to create a feeling of confinement and entrapment, amplifying the characters' feelings of unease and paranoia. The hotel's shifting architecture further blurs the boundaries between reality and hallucination, challenging the characters' perceptions and deepening their descent into madness.

Familial Trauma and Violence:

"The Shining" also explores themes of familial trauma and the cyclical nature of violence. Jack Torrance's troubled relationship with his family, particularly his wife Wendy and son Danny, is fraught with tension and fear. The hotel's influence exacerbates these dynamics, driving a wedge between the family members and fueling Jack's descent into violence. Kubrick's exploration of these themes underscores the film's exploration of psychological horror and the profound impact of isolation on the human psyche.

Symbolism and Subtext:

Throughout "The Shining," Kubrick employs symbolism and subtext to enrich the film's themes of isolation and madness. The use of recurring motifs, such as mirrors, mazes, and the color red, serves to deepen the narrative's psychological complexity and foreshadow the characters' fates. These symbolic elements invite viewers to interpret the film on multiple levels, exploring themes of identity, repression, and the subconscious mind.

Chapter 6: The Shining's Cultural Impact

Beyond its initial release in 1980, Stanley Kubrick's "The Shining" has left an indelible mark on popular culture and the horror genre. The film's unique blend of psychological terror, haunting imagery, and thematic depth has solidified its status as a cinematic masterpiece and continues to captivate audiences and filmmakers alike.

Critical Reception and Box Office Performance: Upon its release, "The Shining" received mixed reviews from critics, with some praising Kubrick's direction and Nicholson's performance while others criticized its departure from Stephen King's original novel. Despite initial reactions, the film has since garnered a cult following and is widely regarded as one of the greatest horror films ever made. Its initial box office performance was moderate, but its influence and cultural impact have grown exponentially over the decades.

Reinterpretations and Homages
"The Shining" has inspired numerous reinterpretations and homages in film, television, literature, and popular culture. Filmmakers and artists have drawn upon Kubrick's visual style, thematic depth, and iconic imagery to create works that pay homage to or reimagine elements of the film. References to "The Shining" can be found in everything from music videos to video games, showcasing its enduring influence on contemporary media.

Fan Theories and Interpretations:
One of the enduring legacies of "The Shining" is its ability to provoke discussion and speculation among viewers. Fan theories about the film's hidden meanings, symbolism, and ambiguous ending continue to circulate online and in academic circles. From interpretations of the hotel's layout as a

metaphor for the human psyche to debates over the true nature of the supernatural forces at play, "The Shining" invites viewers to engage with its narrative on multiple levels.

Influence on Filmmaking and Horror Genre:
"The Shining" has had a profound influence on filmmaking, particularly within the horror genre. Kubrick's innovative use of cinematography, sound design, and narrative structure has inspired generations of filmmakers to push the boundaries of visual storytelling and explore themes of psychological horror and existential dread. The film's impact can be seen in the work of directors such as David Lynch, Guillermo del Toro, and Ari Aster, who cite Kubrick's influence on their own cinematic visions.

Legacy and Enduring Popularity:
More than four decades after its release, "The Shining" continues to resonate with audiences worldwide. Its iconic scenes, memorable quotes,

and complex characters have become ingrained in popular culture, ensuring its status as a timeless classic of horror cinema. The film's legacy is further cemented by its preservation in the National Film Registry and its ongoing relevance in discussions of cinematic artistry and thematic depth.

Chapter 7: Behind the Scenes: Production Challenges

The making of Stanley Kubrick's "The Shining" was not without its challenges, as the film's meticulous craftsmanship and ambitious vision presented unique hurdles for the director and his team. From the construction of elaborate sets to the adaptation of Stephen King's novel, the production of "The Shining" was a journey marked by creativity, innovation, and occasional setbacks.

Adapting Stephen King's Novel:
One of the initial challenges Kubrick faced was adapting Stephen King's novel "The Shining" for the screen. While the novel provided a rich tapestry of supernatural horror and character depth, Kubrick opted to take a more psychological approach, focusing on the themes of isolation and madness. This departure from King's original narrative led to

some controversy among fans of the novel but ultimately contributed to the film's distinctive vision.

Set Design and Construction:

Central to the film's visual impact is the meticulously crafted sets of the Overlook Hotel. Production designer Roy Walker and his team spared no expense in recreating the grandeur and eerie atmosphere of the hotel, from the iconic hedge maze to the sprawling corridors and opulent interiors. The construction of these sets was a massive undertaking, requiring careful attention to detail and a keen understanding of Kubrick's aesthetic vision.

Use of the Steadicam:

A groundbreaking aspect of "The Shining" was Kubrick's use of the Steadicam, operated by inventor/operator Garrett Brown. This innovative technology allowed for fluid tracking shots that captured the labyrinthine layout of the Overlook

Hotel with unprecedented precision and fluidity. The use of the Steadicam in scenes such as Danny's tricycle ride through the corridors became iconic moments in cinematic history, showcasing Kubrick's commitment to pushing the boundaries of visual storytelling.

Working with Actors:

Stanley Kubrick was known for his meticulous approach to directing actors, often requiring multiple takes to achieve the desired performance. Jack Nicholson's portrayal of Jack Torrance and Shelley Duvall's portrayal of Wendy Torrance are marked by their intensity and emotional depth, a testament to Kubrick's ability to evoke nuanced performances from his cast. The dynamics between the characters, particularly the escalating tension within the Torrance family, were carefully crafted through Kubrick's direction and the actors' interpretation of their roles.

Post-Production and Editing:

The post-production process of "The Shining" was equally meticulous, with Kubrick overseeing every aspect of the editing and sound design. The film's haunting score, composed by Wendy Carlos and Rachel Elkind, added to its atmosphere of suspense and unease. Kubrick's attention to detail extended to the film's pacing and structure, ensuring that each scene contributed to the overarching narrative of psychological horror and supernatural intrigue.

Legacy and Impact:
Despite its initial mixed reception, "The Shining" has since become a cornerstone of cinematic horror, admired for its technical craftsmanship and thematic depth. The film's production challenges and creative decisions have contributed to its enduring legacy, influencing filmmakers and artists across generations. From its innovative use of technology to its exploration of psychological terror, "The Shining" stands as a testament to Stanley Kubrick's visionary approach to filmmaking.

Conclusion: The Enduring Legacy of "The Shining"

Stanley Kubrick's "The Shining" stands as a monumental achievement in cinematic horror, renowned for its atmospheric tension, psychological depth, and iconic imagery. From its inception as an adaptation of Stephen King's novel to its release and subsequent cultural impact, the film has captivated audiences and inspired filmmakers for over four decades.

Exploration of Psychological Horror:
At its core, "The Shining" is a profound exploration of psychological horror and the human psyche's darkest recesses. Kubrick's decision to deviate from King's supernatural narrative allowed him to delve deeper into themes of isolation, madness, and the cyclical nature of violence. The film's chilling portrayal of the Torrance family's descent into terror within the ominous confines of the Overlook

Hotel resonates on both visceral and intellectual levels, challenging viewers to confront their own fears and anxieties.

Innovative Cinematic Techniques:
Stanley Kubrick's visionary direction and innovative use of cinematic techniques have left an indelible mark on the art of filmmaking. From the pioneering use of the Steadicam to the meticulous set design and haunting soundscapes, every aspect of "The Shining" is a testament to Kubrick's meticulous craftsmanship and commitment to visual storytelling. The film's iconic scenes, such as Danny's tricycle ride and Jack's "Here's Johnny!" moment, have become ingrained in popular culture, showcasing Kubrick's ability to create enduring cinematic moments that transcend time.

Cultural Impact and Influence:
Since its release in 1980, "The Shining" has continued to captivate audiences and inspire filmmakers across genres. Its influence can be seen

in the work of contemporary directors who draw upon Kubrick's thematic depth, visual style, and narrative ambiguity to create their own cinematic visions. The film's enduring popularity has spawned countless interpretations, fan theories, and homages, cementing its status as a timeless classic of horror cinema.

Legacy and Critical Reception:

While "The Shining" initially received mixed reviews from critics and audiences, its reputation has grown exponentially over the years. The film's inclusion in the National Film Registry and its ongoing relevance in discussions of cinematic artistry and genre-defining horror underscore its enduring legacy. Stanley Kubrick's uncompromising vision and the collaborative efforts of his talented cast and crew have ensured that "The Shining" remains a benchmark of excellence in storytelling and filmmaking.

In conclusion, Stanley Kubrick's "The Shining" continues to haunt and mesmerize audiences with its exploration of psychological terror, innovative filmmaking techniques, and timeless themes. As we navigate the labyrinthine corridors of the Overlook Hotel alongside Jack, Wendy, and Danny Torrance, we are reminded of the enduring power of cinema to provoke, challenge, and inspire.

Appendix: Further Reading and References

1. Stephen King's Novel vs. Kubrick's Film: A comparative analysis of the differences between Stephen King's original novel "The Shining" and Stanley Kubrick's cinematic adaptation.

2. Critical Reviews and Analysis: A compilation of critical reviews and scholarly articles discussing the themes, symbolism, and artistic merits of "The Shining."

3. Interviews and Insights: Excerpts from interviews with Stanley Kubrick, Jack

Nicholson, Shelley Duvall, and other key members of the cast and crew, providing insights into the making of the film.

4. Production Notes: behind-the-scenes photographs, production sketches, and anecdotes detailing the challenges and innovations during the filming of "The Shining."

5. Legacy and Influence: Discussions on the cultural impact of "The Shining," its influence on subsequent horror films, and its place in cinematic history.

6. Fan Theories and Interpretations: A collection of fan theories and alternative interpretations of the film's narrative, symbolism, and ambiguous ending.

7. Further Viewing and Reading: Recommendations for additional films, books, and scholarly works related to Stanley Kubrick, Stephen King, horror cinema, and psychological thrillers.